COLLECTING COMIC BOOKS

A Young Person's Guide

COMIC BOOKS

By Thomas S. Owens

The Millbrook Press, Brookfield, Connecticut

Library of Congress Cataloging-in-Publication Data
Owens, Thomas S.
Collecting comic books: a young person's guide /
by Thomas S. Owens
Summary: A guide for would-be or experienced collectors
of comic books.
ISBN 1-56294-580-7 (lib. bdg.) ISBN 1-56294-904-7 (tr. pbk.)
1. Comic books, strips, etc.—Collectors and collecting—Juvenile literature.
[1. Cartoons and comics—Collectors and collecting.]
PN6714096   1995   741.5′0973′075—dc20   94-48117   CIP   AC

Published by The Millbrook Press
2 Old New Milford Road
Brookfield, Connecticut 06804

CONTENTS

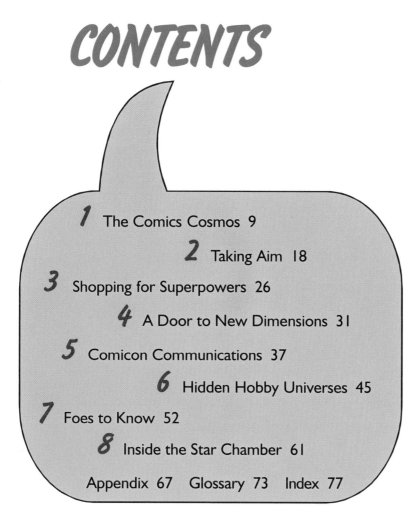

1 The Comics Cosmos 9

2 Taking Aim 18

3 Shopping for Superpowers 26

4 A Door to New Dimensions 31

5 Comicon Communications 37

6 Hidden Hobby Universes 45

7 Foes to Know 52

8 Inside the Star Chamber 61

Appendix 67   Glossary 73   Index 77

This book is dedicated, with thanks, to many friends: author Diana Helmer, editors Elaine Pascoe and Karen Unger Sparks, librarian David Hurkman, collector Thomas Doane-Swanson, and historian Ron Goulart—all super-heroic supporters of comic books and children's literature.

THE COMICS COSMOS

Where did they come from?

The beginnings of comic books can be traced to one birthplace: the daily newspaper.

The Yellow Kid was a mainstay in the New York *Journal*. His 1895 debut marked the wide-scale acceptance of the first comic-strip character. Despite the popularity of "Kid" and other ongoing strips, however, for almost forty years illustrated newspapers were the only way fans of the medium got their regular dose of entertainment.

Things changed in 1934, when *Famous Funnies #1* appeared. Did you miss a few installments of your favorite characters in the newspaper? No problem! The monthly comic book carried reprints of the most popular comic strips.

That first collection of comic strips and all the comics that followed are classified according to the years they were printed. Just like scientists studying dinosaurs, collectors and dealers studying comic books group the issues by certain time periods.

Marvel Comics, which published its first issue in 1939, and Detective Comics (DC) are two of the largest comic-book companies today. Their popular heroes and superheroes are familiar to almost everyone.

The Golden Age of the 1930s and the 1940s featured debuts of major characters and publishers. Superman, created in June 1938 by Jerry Siegel and Joe Shuster, made his first appearance in *Action #1*. Batman came a year later. The two characters were both parts of the DC (Detective Comics) family.

Another comics family, Marvel, launched its first issue in 1939. DC and Marvel have become comics dynasties, known today by hobbyists as "The Big Two."

The Golden Age had already ended when comics fans faced a crisis in 1954. Dr. Fredric Wertham published his book *Seduction of the Innocent,* which claimed to prove that sex and violence lurking within comic books led to juvenile crime and other social problems. Wertham's book was discussed in the pages of many popular magazines.

Publishers feared that the subsequent hearing by a special Senate crime investigating committee, chaired by Estes Kefauver, would lead to laws limiting the types of comic books published. Newsstands and groceries were afraid to sell comic books because the protests of parents might ruin their businesses.

The comics industry reacted by creating the Comics Magazine Association of America. This group's mission was to judge content and award the "Approved by the Comics Code Authority" symbol to acceptable comic books. This seal of approval worked much like "thumbs up, thumbs down" movie ratings. However, a comic book that didn't receive a "thumbs up" would most probably not be distributed at all. Public confidence in comic books was restored, allowing comic books to advance to the Silver Age.

This new era in comic books began in a "Flash." The Flash was actually a 1940s superhero. But his appearance in *DC's Showcase #4* in September 1956 marked the beginning of a more advanced level of art and stories. Originally selling for a dime, the value of this issue was estimated at $12,000 in 1990s price guides. The first of the current Marvel legends bowed in 1961 with the fall issue of *Fantastic Four #1*.

The X-Men, who did not attain superstar status until arriving on the television animation scene nearly three decades later, were born in the summer of 1963.

The Modern Age began with the end of the Silver Age, in early 1970. Some characteristics of the Modern Age include the reduction in the size of comic-book pages by nearly a half inch, and in the appearance of "comics only" stores. Another Modern Age milepost was the 1971 introduction of *The Official Overstreet Comic Book Price Guide*, by hobby leader Robert M. Overstreet. When dealers say they buy and sell at "Overstreet," it means they use the values quoted in his price guides.

The 1970s also brought widespread appreciation of self-published titles. In the 1960s most comic books published by an artist or small group of independents not connected to a major company like DC were considered "underground" works. Often, themes of drug use, violence, or sex made these true "adult" publications.

However, self-published treats such as *Cerebus*, *The Aardvark*, and *ElfQuest* explored themes of fantasy and humor, all without the usual groups of heroes and villains. Appealing to all ages, these comic books earned widespread distribution and prospered throughout the 1980s. In 1984, Kevin Eastman and Peter Laird self-published 3,000 copies of *Teenage Mutant Ninja Turtles #1*. The Turtles's success did not come as quickly as it might have if they had been part of a major company. Or, as the Turtles themselves might say, "Making your own pizza isn't as fast as calling a delivery truck." But Eastman and Laird's homemade comics recipe resulted in popularity that crossed over to movies and TV, even to mainstream comic books.

By the 1990s, the average comic-book price surpassed $2 per issue, up from 15 cents just thirty years before. Publishers and dealers estimated that between $500 million and $1 billion would be spent on comic books every year of the century's last decade. *Comic Buyer's Guide*, a respected weekly publication established in the early 1970s, listed 122 steady publishers in 1993.

Topps, a famous card producer, entered the comics field in 1993 and has created innovations such as double-cover art spreads and full-bleed borderless pages. "Issue zero" refers to an edition that explains the identities and origins of the characters. These superheroes are also featured in an animated TV series.

Don't be fooled by the crowd of creators, though. Of the 122 publishers, less than two dozen were issuing multiple titles on a monthly basis. Many publishers offered three titles or fewer each year, with new issues offered only every two or three months. New small publishers were sometimes unable to publish on a regular schedule due to delays caused by budget problems, busy printers, slow artists, or other problems that a new business would not yet have learned how to handle.

What kinds of comic books are published? Looking at the huge output of DC and Marvel, new collectors might think adventure and hero titles are the only comic-book themes. And it's true that DC and

Comic books are about more than just superheroes. Dark Horse issued a series of fact-based biographies of baseball stars, complete with two trading cards inserted. The three names along the bottom of the cover credit the writer, penciller, and inker.

Marvel have relied on "superhero" themes so much that both publishers have claimed legal rights to the term through a trademark.

Look closer at newsstands and comics shops, however, and you'll see other varieties of comics:

TEEN/HUMOR Archie and his friends have been voted most popular in their comics class since 1942. Instead of heroes and villains with special powers, the teen/humor genre focuses on humans in ordinary, if sometimes silly, situations. Publishers say that younger and female readers start with these titles and advance to the superhero books.

LICENSED CHARACTERS Movie or television cartoons are "rented" to publishers for comic-book adaptations. Archie Comics publishes Sonic the Hedgehog (video-game character), while Harvey Comics has a full line of characters from Hanna Barbera (such as Scooby Doo and the Jetsons) and other cartoons. Harvey was famed in the 1950s for characters such as Baby Huey, Casper the Friendly Ghost, and Richie Rich. These comic books often feature original tales, not just retellings of TV or movie stories. An experiment in

retellings began in the summer of 1994 when Marvel acquired rights to new Disney projects, beginning with a comic version of the movie, *The Lion King*. Breaking from usual practice, the comic book was released weeks before the movie's debut.

TV/MOVIE This group is similar to licensed comics, but with a few twists. Dark Horse Comics has published a variety of Star Wars and Indiana Jones titles. These brand-new stories feature classic characters from the movies. Dark Horse pioneered the "crossover" technique of combining characters with *Alien Vs. Predator*, creating a battle between two science-fiction movie villains who'd never met on the big screen.

In the realm of un-superheroes, "Ren and Stimpy" and "Beavis and Butthead" are examples of 1990s television cartoons that begged for comic-book attention and got it.

Bongo Entertainment Comics was founded by Matt Groening, creator of the popular television cartoon "The Simpsons." With the first Simpsons comic, Groening took the "spinoff" and "tie-in" ideas to new levels. Both of these devices place minor characters in their own comic books. *Itchy* and *Scratchy* (Bart

Simpson's favorite television stars), *Radioactive Man* (Bart's comic-book hero), and *Bartman* (Bart's make-believe identity) are comic titles from Bongo.

TV/movie comics collectors love Bongo. Turn each Simpsons cover upside down, and the back cover begins a one-time story, such as Busman, the adventures of Bart's school bus driver, Otto.

You can't judge a book by its cover. The front cover of Simpsons Comics #3 (left) introduces the main story. Flip the comic over (right) and you'll find the cover for a "backup" story, a takeoff on 1960s secret-agent TV fare.

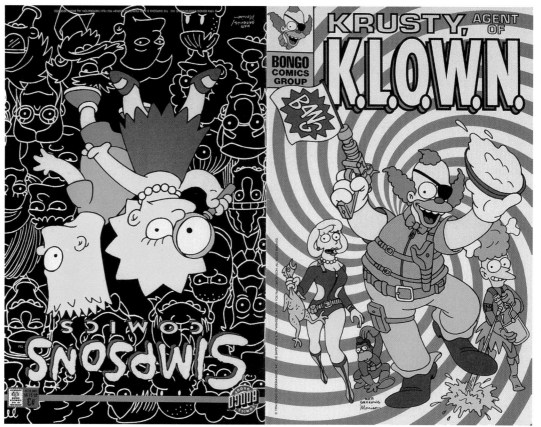

Beginning in the 1960s, readers could find official versions of movies and TV shows, from *The Andy Griffith Show* to westerns and other popular films. To appeal to the most readers, covers would be feature photos of the actual stars, not artwork. Most of the earlier comic books repeated the stories shown on television or in the movies.

Knowing the galaxies of reading choices is your first step in exploring the comic-book universe. To become a true comics collector, however, you'll need to venture into higher realms of knowledge.

TAKING AIM

After choosing the comic book regions you wish to explore, it's time to prepare for the challenges that all comics collectors face.

First, remember that to a collector condition is just as important as content when estimating the value of comic books. A book that is damaged in the smallest way will lose its monetary value because experienced collectors will lose interest.

Comic Buyer's Guide Price Guide, a bimonthly magazine (described in the back of this book), is a noted authority. Each issue contains both a photo rating guide and an illustrated guide to defects with color pictures as examples.

Collector magazines vary a bit in their definition of the condition ratings of comic books. Generally, these are the terms used most often:

MINT "Hot off the press" might be a good description of the top condition. But don't assume that newly printed books sent to subscribers or taken fresh out of the shipping box at the comics shop are mint. When a publisher makes so many issues, a few can slip through with missing pages, mismatched ("off-register") colors, or other printing flaws, which undermine the value of the book.

A mint issue has none of these problems. It looks new and un-touched on the cover, spine, and throughout the book.

NEAR MINT ✳ Tiny printing flaws are allowed, but little wear can be seen. A still-shiny cover and solid spine are required. Older issues are considered "near mint" if only minor signs of discoloration and aging appear.

VERY FINE ✳ These comic books look like they've been read a few times, but are clean and flat. Maybe there's a tiny crease or two, and the cover has lost a bit of shine. Still, a "very fine" issue has no major defects.

FINE ✳ This category of comic book may have corners that are no longer square. The staples in the spine look worn. Yet the cover remains free of serious injuries, and excessive handling is the book's only fault.

VERY GOOD ✳ These comics have visible problems, such as covers torn, creased, dulled by time, or marred by handwriting or a rolled spine.

GOOD ✳ To achieve this status, no taped repairs (which will discolor a comic over time) or pages discolored by constant exposure to light and air are allowed. Likewise, the cover and all pages are intact. Stains and many other signs of wear are common.

FAIR ✳ At least the cover and all the pages are still there. Issues rated fair don't have many good points, due to numerous woes, such as tears, creases, or spine damage. Some demanding collectors ignore issues that are this battered.

POOR ✳ A book ranked as poor may have no cover, missing pages or other serious damage. Most collectors consider these books uncollectible and worthless, but poor books can fill a spot in a collection and provide a good read until a higher quality, more valuable "keeper" is found.

Realize that comic books were not made to last forever. Staples rust, and newsprint pages flake and tear. Collectors have been known to pay restorers more than $1,000 (at $75 per hour) to mend damaged vintage issues.

Does reconditioning pay off? Just ask the auctioneers at Sotheby's. In 1994 a restored issue of Superman's 1938 debut fetched more than $50,000!

While you may not have super-powers, it's possible to protect your mint comics from the ravages of age and wear. For starters, learn to read comic books with gentle care. Do not fold pages while reading. Holding the book by both covers can also damage the spine. Instead, place the comic on a flat surface to reduce tension on the spine. Or rest the comic on the palm of your hand, which takes the pressure off the book's binding.

Although comic books should be stored flat, don't pile them on top of each other. The weight of the stack will curl and crease the bottom few. And always remember to keep your reading and your munching separate. Stains from soda or potato-chip grease can ruin newsprint.

Special boxes with tight-fitting lids are made specifically for storing comic books. These allow the books to be stored standing up for easy viewing, and are narrow enough to keep the book from falling sideways.

Another ally in your preservation battle is "B & B." In hobby language,

"B & B" means "bag and board" your issues.

Plastic bags specially designed to hold comics are available. They come in different sizes for different "Ages," because comic books have been made smaller over the years. Add an acid-free cardboard backing to keep the books from bending or curling. By taping the extra plastic flap behind the cardboard, much like a sandwich bag, you'll be able to remove your books for occasional viewing. Open and close the bags carefully. The tape from the bag flap can accidentally catch on your comic book's cover, and cause damage.

Some cheaper bags will look foggy on their insides after being taped shut for months. The insides of bags made from polyethylene plastic may get as humid as a sauna bath, causing moisture damage to the comic book. Check your collection regularly. To get rid of excess moisture, open the bags every so often so the books can "breathe."

Collectors disagree as to whether or not comic books should be stored within plastic pages in a three-ring binder. Binders always need to be stored upright, because the weight of the books' resting upon each other can cause damage. Also, the comic

books may crease as the plastic holder pages are flipped back and forth, unless cardboard backing is used.

READ TO SUCCEED ✳ Doing your hobby homework means more than buying every new comic or memorizing the newest price guide.

To learn how to spend your collecting money wisely, read a hobby magazine. Although most comics-related magazines don't focus on collecting problems, the news they contain can help you become a better hobbyist and a more appreciative comics reader. A hobby magazine can also provide detailed previews and reviews of the newest comics.

You can go to the newsstand or comic-book shop and try paging through some comic books before making your choice. The adult shopkeeper will most probably not appreciate your spending an entire day reading his comics without buying any, but most shopowners don't mind some intense browsing.

Hobby magazines reveal upcoming story lines, such as the death of Superman. Hobby mags also profile famed writers and artists. You can then look for the comic books featuring the work of these authors and illustrators.

Of course, what's most important is reading the titles and characters you like. Yet value is a consideration in most areas of collectibles. Knowing how much money a comic book is worth helps collectors spend their money wisely and make fair trades with other collectors.

Price guides tell collectors current average retail prices—what collectors can expect to pay when buying a listed item. Prices of collectibles can change quickly, so buyers should always check a recent guide before spending large amounts of money.

Wizard, a popular monthly hobby magazine, prints four pages of abbreviations before each price-guide listing. These codes explain why the comic books are assigned certain values by the magazine. Artists and writers are tracked through the evolution of a title, and their work is noted in specific issues. The comic books done by the original creator of a character tend to gain value more quickly. When a legend like Marvel innovator Steve Ditko is involved, prices jump accordingly.

These creator credits in price guides are welcome aids, considering that some comic-book publishers in the Silver Age and before didn't provide any printed credit to artists and writers.

Likewise, a detailed price guide will note the numbers of issues with crucial plot twists. The death of a character or a character's debut makes books more collectible. Battles between heroes and villains or stories explaining the origin of characters make a comic book gain value more quickly.

How could *The Amazing Spider-Man* #300 be worth four times more than issue #301 or twice the price of #299? The big "three-oh-oh" was only the third issue rendered by future Spawn creator Todd McFarlane. Best of all, the origin of the evil Venom and the return of Spider-Man's traditional uniform of red and blue are highlights of this edition.

FINDING A FIELD ✳ The comics cosmos has countless worlds to explore, but you are just one explorer. Whether you've been given a few older issues by a relative, or you've invested your entire allowance in the comics shop, or you've just begun reading about comics collecting, now is the time to ask yourself: Do I have a hobby specialty?

As with any hobby, knowing what not to collect saves time, money, and frustration. Narrow your focus so

that you can shape your goals and your budget.

Will you zero in on works from one publisher or on lines starring certain characters? Of course, comic books from the Modern Age may seem most affordable, because they are the newest. But do the comic books you can most easily afford feature the stories and art you love?

Some collectors, after reading about famed artists and writers, may vow to pursue all works by these creators, no matter what the titles are. When Jack Kirby died in 1994 at the age of seventy-six, the comics collecting world lost a man who helped create legends like The Fantastic Four, the Incredible Hulk, and Captain America. Collectors paid extra for any work featuring Kirby's work. Many hero-oriented hobbyists have considered adding 1950s true-life (human!) romance comic books to their collections, simply because some titles contain early rare examples of Kirby's work outside the adventure arena.

Some new collectors caught the "investor" fever of the 1990s. The belief was that the premiere of any new title, be it a #1 or a #0 (for an "origin" story discussing the forma-

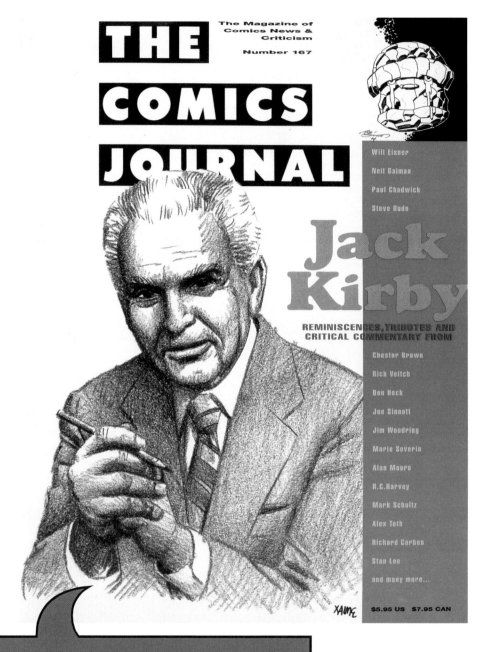

The Magazine of
Comics News &
Criticism

Number 167

THE
COMICS
JOURNAL

Will Eisner

Neil Gaiman

Paul Chadwick

Steve Rude

Jack
Kirby

REMINISCENCES, TRIBUTES AND
CRITICAL COMMENTARY FROM

Chester Brown

Rick Veitch

Don Heck

Joe Sinnott

Jim Woodring

Marie Severin

Alan Moore

R.C. Harvey

Mark Schultz

Alex Toth

Richard Corben

Stan Lee

and many more...

$5.95 US $7.95 CAN

Jack Kirby created legendary comic-book heroes. In the right-hand corner of the cover of this collectible tribute issue, one of Kirby's Fantastic Four characters weeps over the news of the creator's death at age seventy-six.

tion of characters) would bring sure-fire payoffs.

Any collector should be able to do some quick math to get an idea of how costly collecting every "first" is-sue would be. Hobby magazines print preview lists of expected #1 and #0 issues for any upcoming month. Chances are you'll find as many as fifty "new" series appearing each month, meaning the average cost of collecting can reach three figures—$100 or more—each month. Worst of all, many of these struggle for months to rise even $1 over the cover price.

Developing your hobby strengths won't be tough, providing that you don't move too fast. The choices are countless.

Picking a comic-book field that pleases you and suits your reading taste is the surest path to collecting success.

SHOPPING FOR SUPERPOWERS

3

Comic-book collectors are often a loyal bunch who tend to buy their reading material from just one source. But why should collectors care where their comic books are bought?

In the 1950s and 1960s, comics consumers had only two places to shop: the newsstand and vending machines.

At many newsstands, spinning wire racks housed the comic books to keep children from disturbing sup- posedly serious adult customers. (At that time, many store owners didn't realize that adults liked comic books, too.) The wire racks crowded comics buyers together to discourage them from standing around reading for free and possibly damaging the comics.

Yet the store owners actually caused more damage to the books than young browsers did. When the books were unpacked, some news- stands would stamp the date the

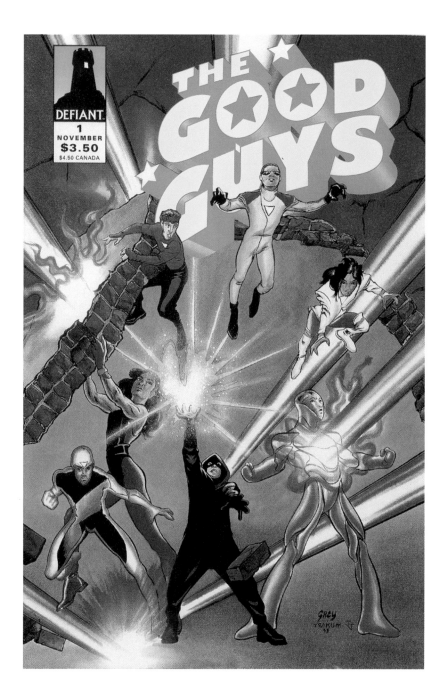

This now-defunct publisher held an essay contest for grade-school students, then created a special issue in which the characters were based upon the actual kids who were chosen as winners. A real-life comics store and artist Rob Liefield were also woven into the storyline. The contest challenged the entrants to explain what they would use their superpowers for, if they had them.

books arrived on each cover. Collectors back then, before price guides and values, didn't realize that years later stamped books would be banned from mint classification.

A rubber stamp can lessen a comic's value, but another old newsstand practice also ruined the dollar value of many past issues.

A newsstand seller used to be able to get refunds for unsold copies from publishers. The publisher required the seller to tear the title section of the cover off the unsold book and mail that piece of the cover back for a refund or for credit on future purchases.

The publisher assumed that the newsstand owner would then throw out the damaged comic. However, some businesses gave away the books, while others sold them at a discount. Although someone who simply wanted to read a new story might not complain about a damaged cover, authors, illustrators, and publishers were being robbed by deceptive comics sellers. Currently, publishers include a note in each issue stating that if the book you bought was reported as "unsold or destroyed," the authors and artists would not receive a royalty payment for the sale.

 ending machines of the 1950s and 1960s were sometimes set up to spit out a comic for a dime or 12 cents. Collectors didn't find this method so heavenly, however. For starters, the machines often wouldn't work or wouldn't be refilled with new issues on time. Also, some comic books got mangled coming out of the machine.

Today, the question of where to buy comic books is still tricky, especially when grocery or department stores sometimes sell titles at a 10 percent discount. Those savings may not seem like such a bargain after you've considered some of these possible problems.

First of all, some retail store managers don't realize that comics collectors care about condition. Stores might stack all their comics titles into one or two piles. The customers must sort through the stacks, bending, wrinkling, and causing wear to each issue just by handling it. Worse yet, some stores will slap gooey price stickers on covers, ruining a book's condition.

Secondly, store magazine racks may not carry all available titles. Limited display space is one reason. Another is the fear of offending consumers if the publisher prints cover art with a violent or sexual tone. An entire department store chain, for example, with branches all over the United States, could refuse to put that title on its shelves. Comics publishers may fear censorship by the government and the public, but their biggest enemies can be the stores that are unwilling to sell anything the least bit controversial.

A huge chain store may also carry only two copies of each title. So if you aren't waiting in the store for the magazine truck to arrive, you may arrive at the magazine rack too late to find what you are looking for.

ail subscriptions are an alternate way to buy comic books. Usually, inside the front cover of your book, or on the facing first page, tiny print will state how many yearly issues are published and how much a subscription costs. A mail-in coupon might be included within the books also. (Don't cut it out! Make a photocopy and avoid ruining the book's mint condition.)

Gone are the days in which a publisher would offer big discounts to subscribers to ensure regular cus-tomers and income. Yet subscribers are still valuable to publishers because subscriber money comes in before the comic books are printed, and that money can be used to pay the printer. That's why subscribers often get discounts that can be as much as 20 percent. Marvel even offers discounts when you get a friend to subscribe.

Although you are guaranteed to get every issue when it's new, comics, like all magazines, occasionally get rough handling when sent through the mail. Don't expect every issue to arrive in mint condition, even though the publishers are doing their best to make their books post-office-proof. (Marvel bags every comic and sends a special illustrated backing board.) Another mail-order drawback is that you must pay in advance for every issue for a year. If your favorite artists and writers stop working on them, or if boring story lines start, you are stuck with those comic books anyway.

Another by-mail source exists. Leading companies, like Wisconsin's Westfield Comics offer subscriptions at discounts far greater than the publishers, and may outclass publishers in packing and shipping new books. In business since 1979, Westfield's only requirement is a $10 minimum purchase, paid in advance. In return, the company sends out a monthly order form, offering virtually anything a comics store would sell. Westfield "culls the books," checking that no defective copies are shipped to collectors. Also, the company shares its freebies from publishers and distributors with customers, passing along posters, pins, trading cards, and other types of promotional materials that are worth collecting.

Companies like Westfield advertise in comics and hobby papers. Buying from them can be a great money-saving plan, as long as you find out beforehand if the company has subscriber rules. Find out how many comics you are required to buy yearly, the minimum you are expected to spend, and if there are any other additional charges. Talk with other collectors to find out if the company you're considering has behaved fairly toward them.

Combining shopping methods is fine, as long as your reading interests and hobby budget are satisfied. Of course, none of these options may compare to the thrill and satisfaction of buying from a comics shop.

A DOOR TO NEW DIMENSIONS

4

Like the Batcave, comics shops sometimes seem to be well-kept secrets. Just remember, the Batcave is near Gotham City, hidden under Bruce Wayne's manor. Comics shops are probably close to your home, too, but instead of being in convenient Main Street spots, comics shops are often found in the upstairs room of small stores or in out-of-the-way neighborhood malls.

Look up "comic books" in the yellow-page business section of the telephone book. Dealers estimate there are more than 6,000 comics shops in America alone. In fact, large publishers like DC often offer to pay part of the costs for comics shops to advertise in the telephone book, provided that the ad states that the publishers' books are sold in the shop.

Comics shops come in all sizes. The biggest appeal is that the customers and the employees like comic books as much as you do. A comics shop is usually stocked with new and old titles, along with comics-related merchandise like models, trading cards, and graphic novels (a fancy name for issues that look and feel more like books than comics).

Small businesses often offer a personal touch. Xanadu Comics in Clive, Iowa, is inhabited by a cat named Bruce Wayne (Batman's alter ego). This feline's fame goes far beyond his name. He appears in television commercials promoting the shop.

Businesses like this small Midwestern shop may focus on a particular type of comic book, such as superhero adventures. Other genres will usually be available too, but may have to be special-ordered.

Owners of comics shops often start out as collectors. Even though running a business may leave them little time to read as many comic books as they would like, the owners and staff of comics shops are often your best local source for current information. They may not know the new details of your favorite stories as well as you, but they frequently know the hobby very well. Use these local resources. Ask plenty of questions.

Some shops offer free preservation supplies with each comic you buy—you get your comic bagged and boarded for no additional cost. Many shops offer subscription services, too, and will reserve an issue of your favorite comic when it arrives so that you never have to worry about missing out.

Still other shops display bid boards. Throughout the week, collectors can come in and write down their offers. In auction style, you can make a bid, and then return and outbid others. At week's end, the highest bidder wins. Sometimes, for a fee based on a percentage of the sale price, dealers will allow you to auction your extra copies. This arrangement is called consignment.

Another advantage to a comics shop is personal service. Suppose you have never read *X-Men*, but learn that a special limited-edition issue will be out next month. Your comics-shop dealer would be able to order an extra copy, at cover price, just for you. All you need to do is ask.

omics dealers can be great guides to comics-related subjects, almost like waiters who suggest the best dishes from the restaurant's menu. Perhaps you have younger brothers or sisters who want to read comics, too. You know they need comic books that are easier to read, and your parents are worried about the violence in some stories. A comics dealer could make a suggestion. For example, *Underdog*, from Harvey Comics is popular with younger readers, and has big print, simple words, and no violence except for balloons that read "POW!"

If your little sister or brother likes fairy tales and fantasy, you might be tempted to get an issue of *ElfQuest* with a cover showing seemingly innocent elves. Ask for the dealer's advice, however, and you'll probably hear that *ElfQuest* sometimes contains stories not suitable for younger readers.

Talking to dealers can be a fascinating and free education. Dealers often have the opportunity to travel to comics conventions and meet the creators of your favorite books. You might see personalized autographs from artists and writers hanging on shop walls or displayed in photo albums. Dealers might even have insights and opinions on possible comics investments.

Many dealers make it a point to look out for their "regulars," customers who give their shop frequent business. They might offer regulars small discounts, or bonus items, such as a publisher's promotional poster of an upcoming title.

Even regulars must remember, though, that dealers need to make a living, and that the costs of running a shop include rent, electricity, wages, and advertising. This is why dealers sell old issues at guide-list prices, but may not pay that price when buying old issues from you. Customers rebuying those comic books would have to pay more than guide-list prices in order for shopkeepers to make a profit. Expect dealers to offer half the price-guide value for most comic books they buy from you and other collectors like you.

Finally, don't be surprised if a dealer's price is a little higher or a little lower than the price guide you're consulting. Remember that price guides are only guides, and in the same month different guides can list different prices for the same comic book.

The small, neighborhood comics shop was challenged in the early 1990s. Successful dealers began opening many stores in one city. Spreading out an inventory of comic books to several stores increased a dealer's opportunity to make a profit. The dealer also appeared to be more powerful and far-reaching than he actually was. "If we don't have it here, we can get it from one of our other stores" was a common comment from multistore dealers.

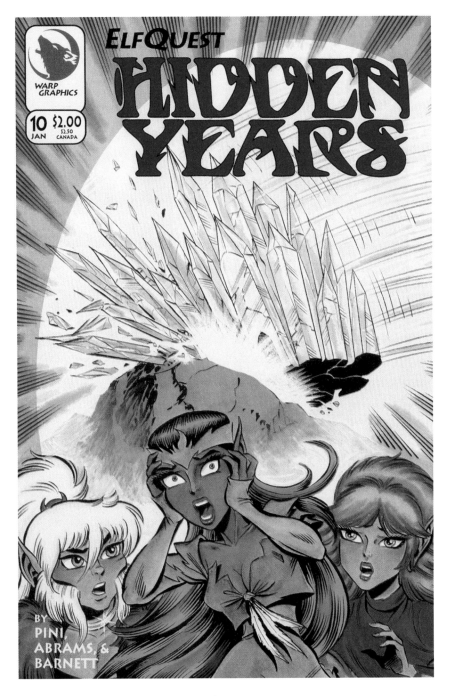

Franchises, outlet stores connected to one huge comics-selling company, may be a future possibility, too. These stores would have the same appeal as fast-food restaurants, with standardized offerings available in every location. Yet a franchise might be as disappointing as a comics rack at a department store. Because profit is the primary goal of most franchises, it's likely that they would sell only the best-selling Marvels and DCs.

In 1994 Marvel threw a scare into comics shop owners. It inserted Marvel Mart, a mail-order catalog into its direct-edition comics (comics only sold at specialty comics shops). These catalogs offered back issues at affordable prices, cheaper than the rates the out-of-print books sold for in comics shops. Some dealers feared that Marvel would stop issuing comic books through shops, and might even open its own stores.

Meanwhile, through all the retail battles, small neighborhood shops keep their customers by fulfilling each customer's needs. Many comics collectors still enjoy being in a place where others like themselves share their enthusiasm for reading, art, and adventure.

But there are other realms that welcome collectors of comics. Many, like the Batcave, are hidden from view. Others are as glaring and bold as the Bat Signal flashing in the sky.

Although ElfQuest books are fantasy comics, the story lines aren't always suitable for very young readers. The word "warp" in the Warp Graphics logo stands for the names of the married couple who created and self-published the books: Wendy and Richard Pini.

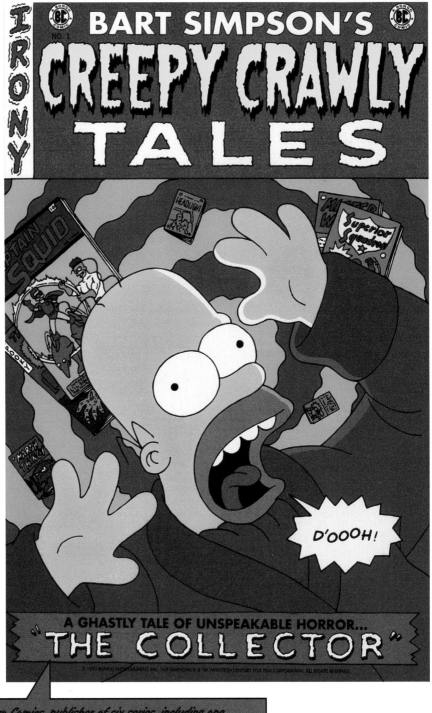

Bongo Comics, publisher of six series, including one based on the characters from "The Simpsons" TV show, is a leader in humor titles. Drawn in the dramatic style of 1950s horror publications, the cover of Simpsons Comics #1 pokes fun at comic collectors.

COMICON COMMUNICATIONS

5

Comicon may sound like a far-off universe, but it's really an out-of-this-world experience every hobbyist should have.

An abbreviation for "comic book collector's convention," a comicon can take many forms. The word dates from 1964, when a collector named Bernie Bubnis organized a New York meeting for fans of science fiction, movies, and comic books. An event lasting a day or less is sometimes dubbed a "mini-con." The longer "cons" can last three to five days, and are held in convention centers and other huge meeting places.

"The San Diego Comic-Con" was started in 1969 by Shel Dorf, who'd been collecting for nearly twenty years. The annual event is still going strong, making it one of the oldest surviving fan rituals.

These days, smaller events are often advertised as "comic book and sports card" shows. The association is made because some dealers have begun to sell both collectibles. In fact, collector cards and comic books have a lot in common. For example, dozens of card sets feature comic-book characters each year, and small wonder: Marvel Comics owns the baseball card company Fleer, and the Topps company produces both sports cards and comic books.

Who goes to a comicon or comics-related sale? Anyone—from collectors to dealers to professionals in the comic-book industry, including writers and artists who help create comic books, as well as people who distribute them to readers like you.

The Chicago Comicon, in its third decade, is one of the best attended, most talked-about events. The 1994 festival featured more than a dozen

Armada created a series of comic books based on Magic Cards, a collectible trading-card game. Dealers, collectors, and manufacturers often combine these two hobbies.

38

group discussions, and an entire room was dedicated to Marvel Comics presentations. The organizing committee noted that collectors had complained because only forty-eight hours of special events had been scheduled the previous year.

Comicons are where folks who never get enough of comic books can come pretty darn close. That's why, before you pack your bags for a large or small hobby fest, it's wise to prepare your game plan. Outlining your goals on paper can help you avoid costly mistakes.

A want list is like a grocery list people make before they go shopping. Write down only the comic books you want to add to your collection, along with notes from price guides as to how much each book might cost.

Once you are inside a convention hall and surrounded by dealers, tempting offers may sway you from your list. Talk of good investments and great values may make comic books you've never read before seem like bargains. In the investment mania, you might overlook the titles you want.

Comicons of the 1990s caught this fever from sports collectors' conventions, where money has become as important as fun. Autographs offer more temptations. Some authors and artists presign postcards with illustrations of their comics characters. Would you rather have an autograph or an issue from your want list? Make that decision before you get in line. Investment fever is why comicon advertisements often boast of dozens of famous writers and artists from the comics industry who will be on hand to sign autographs.

In most cases, creators are paid to sign autographs during a designated time frame, sometimes for less than three hours. In turn, comicon promoters will sell "tickets" allowing attendees the opportunity for one signature.

To get an autograph, you'll be standing in line, with dozens of collectors before and after you. Don't be surprised if you're trapped in an assembly line, shuttled through without a handshake, the time to ask a brief question, or the opportunity to pose for a picture. If you demand extra time, not only could you annoy the "famous-name" guest and the security workers running the signing station, but you'll risk annoying the collectors waiting patiently behind you.

At some events, artists also will agree to create a small number of original sketches to be sold or raffled to attending collectors. The costs of getting autographs or sketches vary from convention to convention. Here's how it works. Usually, an artist or writer is paid a preset fee for attending. Promoters use the money from autograph tickets to pay the guest's fee and travel expenses, such as airfare and hotel costs. Some promoters want to recover only these expenses. Other comicon organizers see autograph signings as huge moneymakers, and demand higher ticket prices for both convention admission and the autographs. Comicon promoters sometimes obtain extra signed comic books and photos from guests, and sell leftovers by mail or at future shows.

The best aspect of hobby events that feature comics creators are the panel discussions they sometimes hold. Hobbyists' questions get answered, artists and writers discuss their careers and accomplishments, and the futures of certain titles and characters are previewed.

Comicons can also offer other types of opportunities. Some comicbook editors and publishers may agree (for free or for a fee) to comment on the work of hopeful comic-book writers and illustrators.

Defiant Company founder Jim Shooter, who had written for DC's *Legion of Super-Heroes* and *Superboy* by age fifteen, added a new dimension to comicons when he began presenting "How to Create Comics." In this seminar, held nationwide at various hobby events, he teaches the basics of creating, writing, and drawing comics to countless collectors.

Smart convention visitors ask about additional presentations before attending. It's possible to write or call a show organizer in advance to learn about autograph policies, publishing forums, and other bonuses. Publishers set up booths and displays at larger cons, sometimes offering posters, sample issues, or other freebies.

The dealer also has a place at the comicon. Although dealers aren't as famous as other professionals in the industry, these hobby brokers are key to expanding your collection.

Some dealers dazzle the public by displaying the newest titles. Itchy readers who don't want to wait for the local shop to acquire the book next week may buy the fresh merchandise quickly, wasting money in-

This 1994 "Superboy Meets Girl" issue of Icon is from the limited-edition crossover series, Worlds Collide. Although other publishers had featured black heroes before, Milestone became known for producing an entire universe of multicultural characters.

tended for "Silver Age" specimens. Stick to your want list.

Don't buy from the first table inside the convention hall. Tour the exhibit area first, noting the booths carrying items from your list. Compare prices and conditions of the older comic books you seek. Dealers with the worst locations, who get the least amount of foot traffic from customers who don't want to walk through the entire auditorium, may discount their comic books more than other dealers.

Professional dealers will greet you by asking "May I help you?" Let them. Tell them you have a certain comic on your want list and ask if they have it. Perhaps they do, but it's not displayed. Ask the price.

More collectors will want a comic in mint condition. Ask if there's a "good" grade of the same book for less money. If you're trying to complete a run of issues, then a book in a less-than-mint condition is a bargain idea.

Some dealers may insist on full price-guide value (or more) for the desired comic. Bargaining for a lower price takes both skill and luck.

If you say that the book isn't that special, you'll only insult the dealer and start an argument. "Take it or leave it" is the standard reply. Negotiating takes patience and timing.

Some dealers will give price breaks during the closing hours of a convention if business was slow. Other sellers might make a deal in the opening minutes of an event, wanting to recover travel costs and rent for the display space immediately.

If you offer to buy several comic books from a dealer, the dealer may be willing to take less money for the entire purchase. Otherwise, your discount may be limited to around 10 percent on a single book. It never hurts to ask politely for a discount. Being told no isn't painful. If a price isn't fair, be polite and leave.

Don't plead for a discount at a crowded table, especially within earshot of other collectors. The dealer knows that other customers will then ask for the same kind of price break, and may say no for that reason.

When you purchase a book from a dealer, be prepared for a surprise. Many dealers don't provide paper sacks for customers. Be sure to bring some sort of shopping bag, backpack, or briefcase to tote your purchases. Otherwise, your acquisition may be damaged before it gets home. At nearly every comicon, one bagless collector will lose a comic he just bought. How? He didn't bring a bag, set the new comic down when shopping at another table, and left it behind as he moved on.

The dizzying experience of a first comicon may cause newcomers to overlook its greatest assets. Those other people clogging the aisles and blocking the tables have a lot in common with you. Many friendships have started at comicons. Who knows? After meeting other comics hunters from your area, maybe you'll join forces and hold your own comicon someday!

THE WORLD'S SNAZZIEST ADVENTURE SERIES!

MADMAN
ADVENTURES

POP ART HEAVEN!

Foil-enhanced covers were popular in the early 1990s. This "ashcan" was from a 1993 Hero Illustrated hobby magazine.

HIDDEN HOBBY UNIVERSES

6

If collectors had superpowers, they'd probably use them to find affordable older issues of their favorite titles. Maybe they'd search for the hidden universes, where Golden and Silver Age editions are free for the asking.

Sound like a fantasy? Actually, even veteran collectors often don't know where to search for cheap or free favorites, but fabulous finds may be close by, waiting for you to discover them.

Start by asking everyone you know if they have any old comics.

Friends, relatives, and neighbors may have piles of titles they don't want. Remember, many noncollectors may think their old comics are worthless.

Your grandparents might see the foil-enhanced covers popular on current issues, and think you'd never care about old fashioned, "regular" comics. If you feel strange asking for comics, think of how much stranger you'll feel when grown-ups tell you that they recycled their old *Superman* comics with yesterday's garbage, sold them at a rummage sale, or simply tossed them out only days before they learned about your interest. "You're too late," are haunting words that comics hunters hate to hear.

Asking could also pay off when visiting teachers, police officers, or anyone working for social or government agencies. New comics may be offered for free by these people, too.

Why? Characters like Supergirl and Spider-Man have starred in public-service comics, specially designed educational titles that are given away to benefit a good cause.

Honda sponsored a *Supergirl* comic that contained a story about wearing seat belts. The company gave away copies at safety fairs, schools, and other places where the public could get the message. Because the DC-produced book wasn't sold in stores, many adult hobbyists didn't find out about the comic until it was no longer available. Meanwhile, kids who had picked up the freebies were able to trade with adult collectors for the comics they wanted instead.

Marvel has created some memorable giveaway comics. *Danger in Dallas* paired Spider-Man with the Dallas Cowboys. *Chaos in Kansas City* joined "Spidey" (fans' nickname for their hero) with the Incredible Hulk. These educational titles were distrib-

uted for free in the cities mentioned in the titles. Dealers now pay $15 and more for copies.

At first, adult collectors ignored giveaway comics. The covers often say "free," and because of their one-time-only nature they weren't part of a larger series. Soon, however, hobbyists discovered that many noncollectors who had been given the books in school or at special events often threw them away after one reading. That's why these "freebies" are often more rare than comic books that collectors pay money for and are more likely to preserve.

An offshoot of the free comic is the fund-raiser. Warp Graphics designed an *ElfQuest* issue for the Make-A-Wish Foundation, with a story suited to that organization. The $2 proceeds went to the charity. Marvel has created limited editions of original stories available only through a mail-in donation. Even with the $5 minimum contribution to organizations like UNICEF, collectors are glad to pay more because they feel that their purchase serves a greater good and that they are making an investment in a unique collectible.

Fund-raiser or giveaway books might appear only occasionally, but comics often appear in other unex-

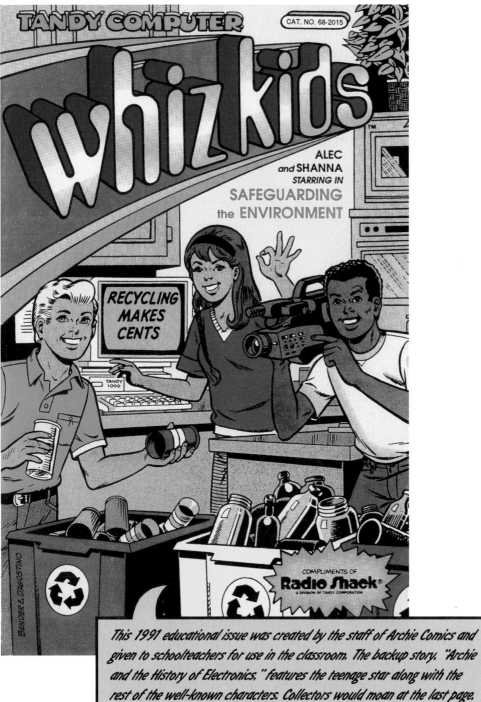

This 1991 educational issue was created by the staff of Archie Comics and given to schoolteachers for use in the classroom. The backup story, "Archie and the History of Electronics," features the teenage star along with the rest of the well-known characters. Collectors would moan at the last page, which proudly announces "This comic is recyclable!"

Free, "giveaway" comics have been a popular form of advertising since the 1950s. This 16-page comic was used to promote the insurance company that sponsored the TV program "Wild Kingdom," as well as the network and stations that aired it.

pected places. Be on the lookout for comic-book bargains in businesses throughout your community.

For years, a popular American pizza franchise has held various comics promotions. Make a purchase, and get a comic. These premium comics were originally reprints and condensations of previously published titles. But, in 1994, the food franchise commissioned Marvel to create four original comic-book adventures.

Using free comic books to increase sales is catching on with other companies, too. When *Batman: The Animated Movie* was released on video, buyers found a special-edition comic enclosed with each videotape.

Don't forget to search in grocery stores, too. Breakfast cereals are famous for offering comic books by mail, in exchange for money and/or proof of purchase. You can't read the whole comic in advance (or get a review of the issue), but these cereal-box offers are hard-to-get items that many collectors ignore. This can be a mistake, because many comics premiums are produced by the same Marvel or DC creators you collect. You could wind up owning a specimen that your friends may be sorry they missed.

Food-premium comic books serve many useful purposes. Even if you've never read about X-Men before, you can sample their adventures through the free titles. You may decide that the world of the X-Men is nice, but you don't want to spend much time there. But your free title may provide you with a unique issue to trade.

iscount stores sometimes acquire merchandise from comic-book shops that are going out of business. Book distributors may buy "remainders," which are unsold editions from newsstands. The same goes for liq-uidation "dollar" stores, those businesses that sell all types of merchandise. Some of these places will have toy sections or bookshelves, and you should explore them all.

Used bookstores are just what the name implies. People sell their used books to the store or trade them in for other well-read books. Comic books can pop up cheaply here, but they're often in poor or fair condition.

Rummage sales or auctions have comics occasionally, but antiques fans scour these places early. People who don't collect comic books may buy them anyway, regardless of the condition, because they assume that anything old must be of value. This is why noncollectors are also sometimes reluctant to part with their old, unread titles.

If you are buying someone else's books, be honest about the possible value. Rate the condition of their books. Use your price guide to show them that titles that are only in fair condition are worth only a fraction of the mint value listed. Explain to them that the list prices are retail estimates of what dealers would charge for those books, but not what dealers would pay.

Many adults won't want to set up

In 1994, DC offered one of four different mini-comics, measuring 2 1/2 by 4 1/4 inches, in specially marked cereal boxes. Some of the stories in these types of premium comics are adapted reprints; others are originals.

tables at comicons or run advertisements to sell the books they have. In fact, many older people have fond memories of their now-grown children once reading those comics. Chances are, if you show how dedicated you are to collecting old books, they might give you a huge price break.

Why? The reason may be they'd be happier with less money if they knew that their comics were going to someone who would enjoy and appreciate them, and not just make money with them, as a dealer would. Imagine yourself selling a favorite book from your collection, knowing that the dealer will sell the book to anyone if he can double his money. You'd prefer a good home for your book, too.

Here's the rule: Be friendly, outgoing, and honest. These are the same attributes that superheroes try to develop and are the ones you should emulate in your comic-book searches.

FOES TO KNOW

Every superhero faces villains and enemies. We like to read about these battles because real life may sometimes seem like a battle, too. Real people can be like superheroes: Both need to know their enemies before they can use their powers to make a battle plan.

Who are the foes of the comic-book collector?

Comics fans aren't likely to find scowling tricksters with evil masks. Instead, those who defeat you in a hobby duel are smiling, ordinary-looking humans.

All a hobbyist needs to triumph over most common pitfalls is a little knowledge. As you journey deeper into the comics world, expect to encounter a few of the following roadblocks along your way:

CABLE SHOPPING NETWORKS

Presto! Right into your home, through the magic of television, come famous creators of comics. There's no need to travel to a comicon or write a letter. Just flip on the TV and you can meet the greats of comics publishing.

They may talk about how they invented your favorite superhero, or they may describe how a popular story line was born. Viewers call in to talk with these comic-book legends.

Meanwhile a host describes some "special" collectibles available for only one hour. Because you are watching the program, you can buy these goodies for a fraction of their price-guide value. Sometimes the publishing-house star will autograph every item sold.

Don't run to ask your parents to call and buy one of everything. After a few minutes, those "rare" items may be discounted even more. Too bad for the overanxious callers who phoned in quickly.

Sure, shop-at-home programs get your attention. However, they're actually endless commercials. When the host comments about "price-guide value," ask yourself what price guide is being used. Don't believe everything you see or hear.

Check your own price guide. Quickly call a collector for a second opinion. It's possible to find good deals on such programs, but use caution.

AUTOGRAPHED EDITIONS Signed comic books became a hobby rage in the 1990s. Getting an autograph by the creator on the actual comic was like owning the next best thing to original art.

Previously, autographed comic books were considered conversation pieces, something to show off and to dress up a collection. Then, when writers and artists starting asking for huge appearance fees to attend comicons, the idea of paying for autographs began.

In the beginning, convention promoters could get some extra issues signed, then sell them later by mail to people unable to attend the event. This helped cover some of the expense of hiring a comics celebrity.

Suddenly, autograph dealers learned that they could make their own signed limited editions of comics. No new issues were printed. Instead, the dealer would ask an artist to autograph and number 1,000 books. Then the ads read, "Signed limited edition of 1,000."

Does this mean that only 1,000 comic books were ever printed? Or would the artist who signed the thousand never autograph that book again in his lifetime? The answers are no and no.

If a *Spider-Man* book is offered in an autographed edition by the artist and writer for $10, is that a rip-off?

The price could be a bargain to a signature-hungry collector. If you were going to travel to a comicon to stand in line and pay for those creator autographs, then your ten bucks could save you the time, admission tickets, and other hassles. But if you think your autographed purchase will triple in value in a month, your dreams may fade quickly.

Like sports-card hobbyists, comic collectors will probably always be in two camps about autographs. Some people believe an autograph increases an item's value. Others believe any writing, even an autograph, is graffiti and decreases value. Only collect autographs if they mean something to you.

BAGGED EDITIONS ✳ When someone wants you to keep a secret, you might hear, "Don't let the cat out of the bag!" Some secrets are a challenge to keep "in the bag." Collectors face a similar challenge when buying comic books sealed in bags by the publisher.

Inside the bag is a prize offered by the publisher. For example, before the Spider-Man animated television show had its first broadcast, Marvel inserted a different cel replica (reproducing art from the TV animation) in six "Spidey" titles. A sixteen-page booklet about the creation of the cartoon topped off the bonus.

Other publishers offer prepackaged comic books with a trading card or poster. Often, these inserted freebies come only in "direct editions," meaning that the publishers give comics shops special packages as a way to lure customers away from discount-filled department stores.

The prize-inside tradition reached new heights in 1994. *Worlds Collide #1*, a key issue in the "crossover" between DC and Milestone characters, featured an amazing insert. The publisher described the idea as "the best cover gimmick ever"—a TOY! A sheet of clingy vinyl reusable stickers picturing all the super characters was included.

So what happens when you rip open that bag and check your prize before reading that comic?

Wait! Check the price guides. Bagged issues of comic books may increase in value faster than the newsstand edition (which have no prize). However, once you open the bag, the value is blown. Keeping the comic entombed in its bag isn't much better. You'll never enjoy the stories or the prize.

So, if and when you buy older, out-of-print "bagged" issues, make sure dealers aren't charging you for a bagged premium if the copy has been opened and its prize removed.

Beware buyers! Because of the enclosed bonus poster, Innovation bagged its first issue of Beauty and the Beast. Unsuspecting collectors, curious about the contents and finding no description on the cover, probably tore open the plastic, letting the resale value "out of the bag."

If you won't fret about ultimate value and really want that freebie, go ahead and purchase it. If you are angry that you can't enjoy the art and words of your book without damaging its resale worth, don't buy it. Then write the publisher and explain your reason. The comics industry listens to what its customers want. Don't expect immediate results, however. Running a business is like running the government. A majority of the people have to cast their voices for change before the folks in charge take notice.

SPECIAL COVERS

Fancy fronts come in creative varieties. The enhanced covers can be die-cut (with a see-through hole, exposing inside art), or given a three-dimensional look with holograms or chromium- or platinum-embossed accents. Sometimes, new art will appear, by way of a two-cover wraparound spread or a gatefold (three cover panels of art).

Publishers may start claiming months before publication that these covers are limited editions—although actual production numbers won't be revealed. Like bagged editions, the special covers are more expensive than standard titles and usually appear only on "directed" comics-shop editions.

Price guides value newsstand edition covers less than fancier covers. Partly, because the enhanced fronts cost more to make. If you're stashing away comics unread in hopes of future riches, special covers might be a good choice. Remember, though, that popularity is a double-edged sword. Because fancy fronts are popular among collectors, more and more are being created each month. Collectors may eventually find it's expensive to buy every special cover that comes out. Prices would plummet as bored buyers fled, shouting, "Not again!" For hobbyists in a hurry, buying the cheaper, basic versions could be the smarter move.

ASSORTED PACKAGES

Visit any huge department store and you'll see a section for magazines, toys, or maybe just for comics, offering these mysterious packs.

"Get three #1 issues!" proclaims one pack. Even beginning collectors know that the first edition of an ongoing title can climb in value more quickly than following installments—as long as the title becomes established and popular. A "grab bag" collection of assorted unknown titles can sometimes be misleading to hobby newcomers.

Another lure by comic repackagers is calling the pack a "set of out-of-print" titles. The label might say, "One of only 50,000 available." A fancy-looking "certificate of authenticity" is included.

These terms can be tricky. A "set" can be anything you want—which means that everyone's definition will be different. The same goes for a certificate of authenticity. When packs promise that only a limited number are available, that doesn't guarantee that only 50,000 of these comic books are available throughout the world. It means that there are 50,000 such books available from that one packager. Many more of the same title may be collecting dust in comics shops across the nation.

Not all department-store assortments are worthless. If you can see through the bag and recognize the name and number of all the titles inside, then you can use a price guide to estimate the true worth of each of the issues. Possibly, you will get a bargain. Still, without knowing all the facts, you're likely to wind up with comic books worth far less than you believed.

Collector friends are a good de-fense against such temptations. Talk with another comics fan before taking a hobby dive. Taking time to think about your purchase will help protect you against wasting your money. If you think you've bought some worthless merchandise, warn your hobby pals about the offer. They'll appreciate learning from your mistake and may help you out the next time.

POLY-BAGS ✷ If a new issue is displayed at a shop in a poly-bag, don't assume that issue is untouched. Shopkeepers can't be every place at once, and a customer might have removed the issue from its bag while browsing and caused some wear in the process. Examine the poly-bag itself: Is it sealed well? If mint-condition comics are important to you, examine the title's cover, too.

MASS-MEDIA ADAPTATIONS ✷ As a comics fan, you are likely to know when a comics hero or story is adapted for movies or television. When this happens to a title you usually read, you'll want to be careful the next time you shop for comic books.

For instance, anyone who watches the TV or movie version of *Teenage Mutant Ninja Turtles* could be

This Archie Comics issue of Teenage Mutant Ninja Turtles is based on the TV cartoon program. The characters and illustrations are not the same as those in the original TMNT comics, published in the 1980s by Mirage.

surprised when trying to buy comics of those characters. Mirage Publishing offers the "original" green crusaders, continuing the work of creators Kevin Eastman and Peter Laird. Archie Comics, however, has a series of *TMNT*, too, but these characters are of the later TV cartoon variety.

If you ask for comic books as holiday or birthday gifts, people who shop for you could make an innocent mistake. To help them (and yourself), always ask for the specific title and include the name of the publisher, issue number, and serial number.

TRADING Young collectors who don't have a large, steady source of income often don't have the money or time to buy everything they want. Trading is an alternative for them. Many collectors stay away from trading because they fear they will be cheated or will make a bad deal. Just remember that knowledge is power. You don't have to be afraid to swap.

Price guides level the trading field, giving traders of different ages and experience a guide to what is fair. The prices in some guides may be higher than those in others, but traders can decide on a price that's somewhere in between.

The trickiest part of trading is the part that isn't found in the price guides, however. How much is the title worth to you? Only you can decide. Perhaps it's a recent issue that hasn't gained much value yet, but the story contains a plot development that will affect the rest of the series (Spider-Man's marriage, for example, which might reveal his "secret" identity).

Perhaps a title you want is written or illustrated by someone you admire, but the person isn't well-known enough to raise the comic's value. You may decide it's worth your while to pay more than your guide says the comic is worth to complete your hobby's goal. And who knows? The artist you admire may yet become famous, and the comic book you "lost money on" will redeem itself someday.

HOME AND SCHOOL Your teachers will most likely not allow you to use comics titles as subjects of book reports. However, collecting comic books is an acceptable topic for other types of classroom presentations. (You could even use this book as a reference.)

You may also find that people with little experience with this hobby might think of comics as simple and juvenile. You know better. Family and friends who may disapprove of comics may be willing to learn the truth. Give them the facts. Encourage them to try one of your favorites, perhaps after describing it for them. Even if they don't become comics fans themselves, they'll appreciate that you shared your interest with them.

Finally, collectors may find that younger brothers and sisters appreciate their comics too much. In these cases, preservation supplies become very important. Don't leave your comic books lying around the house. Keep them bagged, boarded, and boxed.

And, as mentioned before, encourage your younger siblings to start their own collections—of comics or of any stuff—to keep them from innocently shredding your library. You might have some duplicates or comic books in less-than-great condition that you could pass along. They'll enjoy their inheritance even more if you treat what you're giving them as if it were something special. You should also show your younger siblings how to take care of a collection. Someday, they may be reading right beside you.

INSIDE THE STAR CHAMBER

8

Parents like to tell their children, "We were young once, too." Comics creators might say the same thing to the collectors. In fact, they might add, "We were collectors once, too!"

In fact, talk to anyone working in comics publishing today, and chances are they'll admit that they learned their craft as kids, studying hundreds of comics throughout their childhoods.

Alan Light was a high school student in 1971 when he started publishing *The Buyer's Guide*, a hobbyist publication that grew into the respected weekly *Comic Buyer's Guide*. In 1994 a group of high school students formed Xero Comics, their own publishing company. People like these remind comics creators that the future of their trade is linked to keeping hobbyists happy, and that's why publishers pay attention to letters and comments from customers like you. Most publishing employees make regular appearances at comicons, in order to get feedback from the public.

Greg Goldstein, publisher of Topps Comics, realizes how much companies depend on readers. As Topps expanded its decades-old business from collector cards to comics in 1993, Greg hit the hobby road. He visited comicons, shops, and other locales where he could discover what the buying public wanted. Another part of his mission was to spread the word that comic books aren't just for kids.

Sixty years after the first book of comics appeared in America, Goldstein noted: "The United States is one of the few countries where comics have not been acceptable reading for adults." Goldstein, like other adult comics fans, defended comics as being "as sophisticated as many movies," and noted that renowned filmmakers George Lucas and Steven Spielberg both cited a love of comic books as an early creative influence.

Goldstein compared comics to another film medium, animation. Early Warner Brothers cartoons of popular characters such as Bugs Bunny were originally created for adults. Over the years, these cartoons became a medium for children. But when children grow up and watch those old cartoons again, they will very likely understand lines and actions they didn't when they were small. In other words, cartoons—like comic books—often entertain many ages at once.

This explains why Goldstein and other comics creators have trouble visualizing their audience—and why fan feedback is so important. Goldstein said that reader age varies with every series and its subject matter. Speaking of Topps's movie adaptations of the 1990s, Goldstein pointed out that "*Dracula*'s readers were eighteen through thirty, and *Jurassic Park*'s may have been younger, from twelve to twenty."

Finally, Goldstein confirmed that fans don't need to write complaints in a letter in order for them to be heard. If a current investment mania, such as die-cut, hologram, or foil-embossed covers don't impress you, don't buy those issues. Publishers print what sells, Goldstein says.

hat collectors call "The Marvel Age" began in November 1961, when *Fantastic Four* #1 was issued. Present-day Marvel editor, Steve Saffel, was born just five years earlier, in 1956. In a way, he "grew up" at the same time the famed publishing company did.

Topps's Mars Attack began in 1962 as a collector-card set based on the theme of the book War of the Worlds. The creator was 18-year-old Len Brown. who became the company's creative director 32 years later.

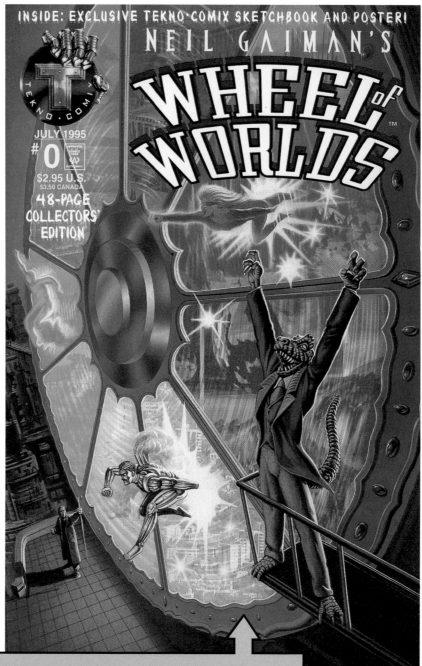

Every year, new comic-book publishers join the scene. Tekno•Comix™, a division of BIG Entertainment formed in 1994, created this "origin" issue, which includes six pages of the artists' preliminary sketches of the characters.

"I don't remember the first comic I ever read, but I remember some of my first Marvel titles," Saffel recalled, listing *X-Men #9*, *Fantastic Four #32*, and *Avengers #9*. "My parents would buy them for me Sundays at the newsstand when they went for their newspaper."

A number of Saffel's childhood friends shared his interest in comics. He managed to keep in touch with only one of them, a junior high pal who turned up at Marvel more than two decades later to help create the *Hokum & Hex* series. Saffel's teenage buddy was Frank Loveche.

Saffel first arrived at Marvel in the late 1980s, before Modern Age comics creators began facing the mass-marketing challenges that movie and television adaptations would later create. He began as an assistant promotions manager, who helped organize informational projects, such as Marvel's "entertainment magazines." Saffel's journalism background combined with a childhood spent reading Marvel comics helped prepare him for his career, he said.

After ten years of observing Marvel customers of all ages at comicons, Saffel noted that he'd seen one big change in hobby attitudes. "There's more focus on value," he said in 1993.

"I think that's a shame. The greatest value I know is the enjoyment of the characters, artwork, and story lines."

Some of the projects that Saffel helped create were inexpensive yet informative works, like the ongoing monthly *X-Men Index*. Still he didn't want to be labeled a historian or an educator of Marvel collectors. "We do what we think will entertain readers," he insisted. "If education happens, it's not a conscious effort on our part."

He did agree that every Marvel title "is a cumulative effect of all that's been done before," meaning that the results of character histories and past adventures influence future stories. Therefore, knowing how individual superheroes evolved will encourage new readers. "The people who work on these books are fans, also," he pointed out. "This piques their interests, too."

When asked to summon his Marvel superpowers to predict the future of the hobby, Saffel declined. Will the emphasis on investments in comics lessen? "I don't know, but I hope so," he said. "The hobby is undergoing a great deal of change right now."

Greg Goldstein of Topps Comics agreed, but added, "This is a good time to be a comics fan."

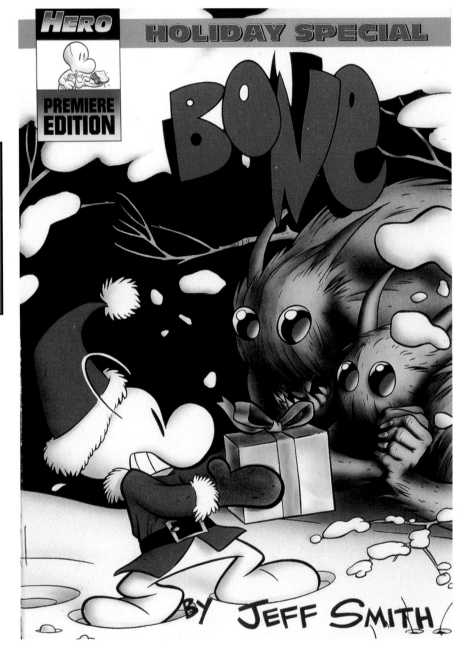

Even though there are no superheroes and the artwork is not in full color, Bone is a self-published hit. This sample issue was a free bonus in a 1993 issue of Hero Illustrated.

APPENDIX

You can learn a lot about comic books by reading comic books.

For instance, there's no need to buy a special book of authors' addresses in order to write to your favorite artists and writers. Simply thumb through the comic book. Somewhere, in fine print, is the address of the publisher. Just be sure that your envelope to the creator is addressed "in care of" the publisher, and that you include a stamped self-addressed envelope for the reply.

For general updates on hobby happenings, collector publications are often your best bet to stay informed about the hobby:

Comic Buyer's Guide (700 E. State St., Iola, WI 54990). This weekly dates from the 1970s, and its black-and-white contents may scare off new readers. Yet advanced hobbyists see *CBG* as a priceless tool, with extensive lists of upcoming shows and classified advertisements.

Wizard: The Guide to Comics (151 Wells Ave., Congers, NY 10920-2064). Just check the covers, and it's obvious that superheroes get the bulk of the ink here. There's coverage on how to find employment in the industry and how to publish your own comics in every issue. Full color throughout, *Wizard* is a whiz at covering anything related to comics—from video games and trading cards to toy models and action figures.

Hero Illustrated (Warrior Publications, 1920 Highland Ave., Suite 222, Lombard, IL 60148). This monthly is accused by some collectors as being a *Wizard* clone. More collector tips seem to slip into *Hero*, although the editorial focus is on superheroes, upcoming issues, and publishing industry news remains.

Comic Buyer's Guide Price Guide. Published six times yearly by the Wisconsin-based *CBG* staff, this doesn't have half the eye-popping appeal of *Wizard* or *Hero*. Instead, *CBGPG* has straightforward text that can be of most help to collectors. "Publisher Spotlight" is written by various comics companies, who provide their own histories. A three-page color photo guide shows the grades and conditions of assorted comics, an invaluable tool ignored by other hobby giants. The *CBG Annual* is a yearbook-style offering that is great for beginners. Articles sum up big events in the comics world during the past year, with special attention paid to comicons and other hobby news.

Comic Book Collector (990 Grove St., Evanston, IL 60201). This isn't as dazzling as hobby competitors. The price guide includes more types of comics than other publications. *Archie* comics and other non-superhero titles ignored by most of the comics media get their own value listings here.

The Comics Journal (7563 Lake City Way NE, Seattle, WA 98115). Hobby news takes a back seat in this sophisticated, adult publication that analyzes the medium. Subtitled *The Magazine of Comics News and Criticism,* the publication isn't recommended for collectors under high school age, due to profanity and graphic commentary on issues of sex and violence. Still the magazine is famed for detailed creator profiles and in-depth information on publishing trends. If a teen student wants to prepare a speech or term paper on the comics industry, TCJ and its back issues are great research tools.

Added bonuses in most hobby magazines are monthly contests and premium inserts. Publications like *Wizard, Hero,* and *CBGPG* are bagged to secure a sample comic, poster, or trading card issue.

To get a taste of how dedicated fans feel about their favorite titles, try reading a fanzine (short for "fan magazine.") Some hobbyists call these "funzines," because fans believe that comics are for fun, not investment. Some fanzines are one-person creations, more like newsletters than newsstand publications. Although their looks might not rival *Wizard* or *Hero*, fanzines are stuffed with specific information you might not find elsewhere.

Two popular fanzine choices are:

The Duckburg Times (3010 Wilshire Blvd. #362, Los Angeles, CA 90010). This publication covers Disney-related comics, including the current Gladstone collections.

The Harveyville Times (1464 La Playa #105, San Francisco, CA 94122). This fanzine reports on the company responsible for the characters Richie Rich, Little Lulu, Casper the Friendly Ghost, and other superhero alternatives.

Of course, other hobby periodicals exist, and new ones may pop up monthly. Keep an eye on newsstands and hobby shops for new entries.

Besides newsstands and hobby shops, wholesalers and discount subscription services exist for new titles. One is Westfield Comics (8608 University Green, P.O. Box 620470, Middleton, WI 53562-0470), one of the oldest and biggest in the business. Competitors abound and can be found advertising in comics and hobby publications.

What about price-guide books? These may not be as helpful as hoped. Even though publishers claim these books are updated yearly, the amount of time needed to prepare and print these books means that the information and pricing inside can be up to two years old. If you've hung around the comics shop much, you know that values change by the week, not just by the year.

The best part of a price-guide book is its checklists. Valuable issues may be described in more detail than in a magazine. Often, magazines print only the most valued past titles. Little-known comic books, often the ones that are still affordable, may be left out of the monthly magazine pricings.

For instance, in 1994, Krause

Publications issued *Marvel Comics Checklist and Price Guide, 1961 to the Present* ($16.95), edited by the *CBG* staff. This info-stuffed volume offers 256 pages of details on all Marvel goodies, from comic books to trading cards to toys. Although the prices might not be too accurate a decade from now, the checklists will remain priceless for studying Marvel history.

Understanding Comics, (Harper Perennial, 1994, $20), written and illustrated by Scott McCloud, does little to help collectors acquire more comics, but it enables all hobbyist readers to get greater enjoyment out of every title in their collections. Some may call this entry the world's longest graphic novel, at 200-plus pages. Actually, *Understanding Comics* is a lively textbook in disguise. McCloud, drawn as a cartoon character, hosts a page-by-page tour of various comics, showing how devices such as thought balloons and splash panels work. If your parents, teachers, or other closed-minded adults you know think that all fans of comics are wasting time, beg them to look at this visual feast.

While most comics-history titles, many available in your public library, build great appreciation for your favorite characters, one book does

more. *A Century of Women Cartoonists* by Trina Robbins (Kitchen Sink Press, 1993, $16.95, paperback) is vital reading for any collector, male or female. Robbins, who has helped create titles for Marvel, DC, and other publishing heavyweights, shows that women possess a past, present, and future in comics publishing. Due to the book's influence, watch for price guides to start giving more attention to old and new books by female creators.

Strangely, most comics-related books still reflect the content of the hobby magazines. Interviews with comic-book writers, artists, and publishers remain the mainstay, along with histories of certain characters. The field of comic books, unlike other hobbies, has been slower to educate collectors. While Kitchen Sink Press has been a trendsetter in insightful comics retrospectives and histories (including the first edition of *Understanding Comics*), publishers don't seem excited about documenting the evolution of the hobby.

A rare exception is *Collector's Guide to Comic Books* by John Hegenberger (Wallace-Homestead Book Company, $12.95, paperback, 221 pages). This 1990 publication, aimed at adult beginners, devotes considerable space to the financial aspects of the hobby. The author financed his college education by selling comics.

Still, until hobby-related publications increase, collectors may need to have a do-it-yourself attitude. Read all you can, but ask questions, too. Nearly all dealers and collectors will be willing to help you learn. After all, everyone was a beginner at one time. Right?

Crossover comics feature guest characters in another star's comic.

GLOSSARY

album. 1. A three-ring binder that holds comics in protective pages. 2. A collection of related stories published within one cover.

annual. An extra-long edition printed once a year, sometimes containing reprinted material, always featuring the first appearance of a character.

arc. The number of issues needed to tell one story, such as the death and revival of Superman.

ashcan. Black-and-white comic books meant as samples or previews, some-times smaller or bigger than the actual publications.

bag. A specially designed, clear vinyl container used to protect comics.

board. An acid-free protective cardboard backing inserted behind a bagged comic, to prevent creasing and spine damage.

book. An abbreviation for "comic book."

cameo. A tiny, sometimes unidentified, guest appearance by a character in a comic.

CBG. *Comic Buyer's Guide*, a weekly hobby journal.

code. Books with approved themes and content, as judged by the Comics Magazine Association of America. See "pre-code."

collection. 1. An assortment of comics owned by one collector. 2. One comic, often oversize, featuring numerous stories, or several comics reprinted into one book or graphic novel.

colorist. Person who colors the illustrations in a comic book.

comicon. Short for "comic book convention"; also known as "con."

Comics Magazine Association of America (CMAA). The governing body of publishers who censor comics for sex, violence, or other controversial elements. Today, more than half the comics printed have not been submitted for approval.

comic strip. A daily installment in a newspaper. A color strip runs in the larger, Sunday "funny papers."

convention. A gathering lasting anywhere from one day to one week, at which fans meet to buy, sell, trade, and meet dealers and members of publishing staffs from the comics industry. Also called a comicon.

creator. Person known for inventing certain comic characters.

crossover. The sharing of one comic by two characters, each from a different title and often from a different publisher.

DC. Stands for Detective Comics, Inc. The publisher, known for *Superman*, *Batman*, and other famed titles, is named for one of its earliest books, *Detective Comics*. The oldest company still in existence, dating from 1935, and originally known as National Allied Publications, DC is now owned by Warner Brothers.

direct. A way of offering editions directly to comics specialty shops, on a nonreturnable basis. These editions, containing special covers, posters or other bonuses, may vary from issues offered in standard retail outlets like newsstands. Some comics may be available only "direct," with issues sold only through hobby shops.

edition. 1. One specific version of a comic, such as a "direct edition" intended only for comics shops, which may have a cover different from other printings of the same comic.

2. From a certain print run, such as "First Edition, one of ten thousand."

editor. Person who oversees writers and artists, supervising the overall creation of a comic.

first appearance. A comic in which a hero or villain is first identified.

Golden Age. Beginning of superhero fare with Superman's debut in 1938, followed by Batman in 1939.

grade. The physical condition of a comic book. Grading determines a comic's monetary worth from "mint" to "poor."

graphic novel. A debated term, possibly meaning a story longer than the traditional twenty to twenty-eight pages. The phrase hints at finer printing and binding methods, as well as a more sophisticated theme.

hero. The comic's protagonist, one who fights for right. Capitalized, the term refers to a monthly hobby magazine, *Hero Illustrated*.

Image Comics. A comics company made up of former DC and Marvel writers, who formed it in order to develop new characters and retain full legal rights to their creations.

independent. A small publisher, sometimes a one-person operation.

inker. Person who outlines pencil-sketched comics pages in preparation for printing, often giving the pencil sketch more detail.

limited series. A story line that the publisher guarantees will end in a predetermined number of issues. For example, part 1 of 3 on the cover indicates a limited series.

Marvel Comics. This company began publishing comics in late 1939. It was once known as Timely Comics, but the name was changed to Marvel Mystery Comics by the second issue. Collectors consider the 1961 debut of the Fantastic Four as the official beginning of the modern Marvel company.

one-shot. A comic, or story line, intended to run for only one issue.

original art. Often, pencil or inked page designs, submitted before the color is added and the book nears printing. They are hard to find, expensive collectibles.

origin issue. An issue numbered #0, in which the history of a hero is explained. This issue is not necessarily the first time a character would have appeared in print.

overstreet. Refers to a price or prices listed in The Comic Book Price Guide by Robert Overstreet, usually quoting estimated comics values from his publication.

panel. 1. A portion of a comics page or daily strip in which words and text are boxed off with borders to show specific action. 2. A group presentation and discussion held for comicon audiences.

penciller. Person who sketches a comic book.

pencils. The initial pencil sketches, which are the beginnings of comic-book art.

premium. 1. An undefined hobby adjective used to describe the merits of a comic, such as enhanced cover or special contents. 2. A prize enclosed in a bagged edition of a comic, such as a free poster or trading card. 3. A type of comic given away at restaurants or groceries offered as a bonus to increase sales.

Seduction of the Innocent. A 1950s book by Fredric Wertham, which claims that comics corrupt America's youth with themes of sex and violence. Wertham was the most famous voice among many raised against some comics themes at this time. His words led to congressional investigations and self-censorship through the CMAA code.

Silver Age. The era of comic-book publication beginning with the reappearance of 1940s hero The Flash in Showcase #4 from DC Comics, in October 1956. The era gave way to the "Modern Age," starting approximately in 1970.

splash panel. Not always the first page, but the page announcing the title of the story. Usually the names of creators (artist, writer, editor) are included.

story line. The ongoing story of a comic book, which may not be told completely in one issue.

INDEX

Aardvark, The, 12
Action #1, 11
Alien Vs. Predator, 15
Animation, 62
Archie, 15
"Archie and the History of Electronics," 47
Archie Comics, 15, 47, 58, 59
Armada, 38
Assorted packages, 56-57
Auctions, 49
Autographed editions, 53-54
Autograph signings, 39-40
Avengers #9, 65

Baby Huey, 15
Bag and board, 20
Bagged editions, 54-56
Bartman, 16
Batman, 11
Batman: The Animated Movie, 48
Beauty and the Beast, 55
"Beavis and Butthead," 15
Bone, 66
Bongo Entertainment Comics, 15, 16, 36
Breakfast cereals, 49, 50
Brown, Len, 63
Bubnis, Bernie, 37

Bugs Bunny, 62
Buyer's Guide, The, 61

Cable shopping networks, 52-53
Captain America, 23
Cartoons, 62
Casper the Friendly Ghost, 15
Century of Women Cartoonists, A
    (Robbins), 70
Cerebus, 12
Certificate of authenticity, 57
Chaos in Kansas City, 46
Chicago Comicon, 38-39
Collector's Guide to Comic Books
    (Hegenberger), 70-71
Comic Book Collector, 68
Comic Buyer's Guide, 12, 61, 67
Comic Buyer's Guide Price Guide, 18,
    68, 69
Comicons, 37-40, 42-43, 53
Comic shops, 31-33, 35
Comics Journal, The, 68
Comics Magazine Association of
    America, 11
Condition of comics, 18-19, 21
Conventions, 37-40, 42-43, 53
Crossover comics, 12, 72

Danger in Dallas, 46
Dark Horse Comics, 14, 15
DC (Detective Comics), 11, 13, 31,
    46, 49, 54
DC's Showcase #4, 11

Defiant Company, 40
Department stores, 28, 29
Direct editions, 54
Discount stores, 49
Ditko, Steve, 22
Dorf, Shel, 37
Duckburg Times, The, 69

Eastman, Kevin, 12, 59
ElfQuest, 12, 33-35, 46

Fair condition, 19
Famous Funnies #1, 9
Fantastic Four, 23
Fantastic Four #1, 62
Fantastic Four #4, 11
Fantastic Four #32, 65
Fanzines, 69
Fine condition, 19
Flash, The, 11
Fleer, 38
Food-premium comic books, 49
Franchises, 35
Fund-raiser comics, 46

Giveaway comics, 46
Goldstein, Greg, 62, 65
Good condition, 19
Grocery stores, 28
Groening, Matt, 15

Harvey Comics, 15, 33
Harveyville Times, The, 69

Hegenberger, John, 70-71
Hero Illustrated, 44, 66, 68, 69
Hobby magazines, 22, 25, 70
Hokum & Hex, 65

Icon, 41
Incredible Hulk, 23, 46
Indiana Jones, 15
Itchy, 15

Jetsons, 15

Kefauver, Estes, 11
Kirby, Jack, 23, 24
Kitchen Sink Press, 70
Krause Publications, 69-70

Laird, Peter, 12, 59
Legion of Super-Heroes, 40
Licensed characters, 15
Liefield, Rob, 27
Light, Alan, 61
Lion King, The, 15
Liquidation "dollar" stores, 49
Loveche, Frank, 65
Lucas, George, 62

Mail subscriptions, 29-30
Make-A-Wish Foundation, 46
Mars Attack, 63
Marvel Comics, 11, 13, 15, 29, 35,
    38, 39, 46, 48, 49, 54, 62, 64,
    65, 70

*Marvel Comics Checklist and Price
    Guide, 1961 to the Present*, 70
Marvel Mart, 35
Mass-media adaptations, 57-59
McCloud, Scott, 70
McFarlane, Todd, 23
Milestone, 41, 54
Mint condition, 18-19, 29, 57
Mirage Publishing, 58, 59

Near-mint condition, 19
Newsstands, 26, 28
New York *Journal*, 9

*Official Overstreet Comic Book Price
Guide, The*, 12
Origin story, 23
Overstreet, Robert M., 12

Poly-bags, 57
Poor condition, 19
Premium comics, 48-50
Price guides, 18, 22-23, 49, 53,
    59, 69

Radioactive Man, 16
Remainders, 49
"Ren and Stimpy," 15
Richie Rich, 15
Robbins, Trina, 70
Rummage sales, 49

Saffel, Steve, 62, 64

Scooby Doo, 15
Scratchy, 15
Seduction of the Innocents,
    (Wertham), 11
Shooter, Jim, 40
Shopping for comics, 26, 28-33,
    35
Shuster, Joe, 11
Siegel, Jerry, 11
"Simpsons, The," 15, 36
Simpson's Comics #1, 36
Sketches, 40
Sonic the Hedgehog, 15
Spawn, 23
Special covers, 56
Spider-Man, 23, 46, 54, 59
Spielberg, Steven, 62
Sports cards, 14, 37-38, 54
Star Wars, 15
Storing comics, 20, 22
Subscriptions, 29-30
Superboy, 40
"Superboy Meets Girl," 41
Supergirl, 46
Superman, 11

Teenage Mutant Ninja Turtles, 12,
    57-59
Teen/humor genre, 15

Tekno•Comix, 64
Topps Comics, 12, 38, 62, 63, 65
Trading, 59

Underdog, 33
Understanding Comics (McCloud),
70
UNICEF, 46
Used bookstores, 49

Vending machines, 26, 28
Very fine condition, 19
Very good condition, 19

Warner Brothers, 62
War of the Worlds, 63
Warp Graphics, 35, 46
Wertham, Fredric, 11
Westfield Comics, 29-30, 69
Wizard: The Guide to Comics, 22, 68
Worlds Collide #1, 54

Xanadu Comics, 32
Xero Comics, 61
X-Men, 11, 49
X-Men #9, 11, 65
X-Men Index, 65

Yellow Kid, The, 9